A Patch of Sunshine

A Collection of Poetry
by John Duel

Library of Congress Control Number: 2015908137
CreateSpace Independent Publishing Platform,
North Charleston, SC

ISBN-10: 1512068314

ISBN-13: 978-1512068313

A Patch of Sunshine is dedicated to Ed McGowan, who graced this earth from March 29, 1962 to January 26, 2015.

He is sorely missed.

Contents

Preface..9

Prologue

I've sung the song of "Sunshine"..............................11

        Sensing Sunshine...12

Part 1

One extra dollop of attention..................................13

        Doors..14

        Kisses..15

        5 a.m. 15

        Math (of Love)....................................16

        Force (of Love)....................................16

        Velocity (of Love)................................16

        Everything My Heart Desires.................17

        Wordless..17

        A Leap Worth Taking...........................18

        Parallel Universes...............................19

        Unshareable.......................................20

        Unraveling Like a Bad Movie.................21

        Chinese-Water-Torture Love.................22

        Sidewalk Artwork...............................23

        Signs...24

        The Great Divide................................25

        Poetry Sublime..................................26

        Deep Questions..................................27

        Addiction...28

Part 2

So many mouths to feed that year...........................29

        The Cloak of History...........................30

        The Great Escape...............................31

        Hungry Henry....................................32

        My Father's First Car..........................33

        Never Again.......................................34

        Vonnie's Husband..............................35

        Potatoes..36

        Carrots..37

        Beets..38

        Trish Gets Her Wish............................40

        Mom's ZZ Top Top..............................41

Part 3

Applause from the sky...................................43

Poetry Barker..............................44

BBQ...44

Workday Blues.............................44

Big Bang..................................45

Creationism...............................45

Our Universe..............................46

Earth.....................................46

Lake and Rock.............................47

Time and Tide.............................47

Thunderclap...............................47

Sunshine..................................48

#16 Dream.................................49

Fallacy #3................................49

Trust.....................................50

Selfie....................................50

Lord of the Ring Trilogy..................51

The Pompous Arrogance Prevalent in
    Thinking an Epic Saga can be
      Reduced to a Haiku.....................51

Styx and Stones...........................52

Still Art.................................53

Screenplay................................54

Novel.....................................54

First Drafts..............................55

Unfinished Business.......................55

Lifelong Joy..............................56

Success...................................56

Beautiful Music...........................56

Part 4

What happened to the little boy?.......................57

Photograph 58

New Life..................................59

Room to Grow..............................60

Memories..................................61

Childhood Recaptured......................62

100 Birthdays.............................62

The Stranger..............................63

State of Mind..63

Ageism...63

87..64

Dust to Dust..65

Eileen..66

Eulogy...67

Unknown Territory...68

Normal...68

The Greatness of Ed.......................................69

In Absentia..70

Grief..71

Hide and Seek..71

Death...72

Valentine Vases...72

The Crime of Wasting Time...............................72

Part 5

Gurgle, gurgle, burp, burp, gurple...............................73

Political Animus...74

A Nation Divided...75

Big Fish...76

FAQ..77

Mid-Life Crisis..77

Rambling Treadmill Thoughts.............................78

Jokes...79

Puns..79

A Glaring Example..80

Breaking Down Poetry for the Uninitiated....81

Attack of the Zones...81

Online Ideal...82

The Meaning of Life Succinctly Explained
        in Seventeen Syllables......................82

Part 6

With hopes to be immortalized...................................83

Blank Page...84

Rejection...85

Procrastination..86

Michelle Pfeiffer..87

American Dreaming...88

Hurricane..89

Cat and Mouse..89

Queen of Hearts.............................90
Poker.............................91
River Bet.............................91
Advice for Playing Tight.............................91
Advice for Playing Loose.............................91
Hope Springs Eternal.............................92
Observe the Acrobat.............................93
Line.............................94

One Liner.............................94
Poverty.............................95
What Would Jesus Do?.............................95
In the Eyes of God.............................96

Part 7
Beyond the barriers of time.............................97
A Lover's Gaze.............................98
Something Simple.............................99
Frozen Image.............................99
On Writing Uninspired Poetry.............................100
Pieces (of the Whole).............................100
Picture Perfect.............................101
Diverging from the Core.............................102
Beautiful You.............................103
Lessons of Love and Lust in Four Parts.........104
Perpetual Motion.............................105
Lonely.............................106
Save Yourself Some Time.............................107
Our Lost Love.............................107
In the Day.............................108
Life with the Bates.............................109
Everything.............................110
Smile.............................111

Preface

Ed McGowan loved my writing. Ed was one of the handful of people who read everything I wrote and did more than anyone to promote my writing. At least one dollar from each copy of *A Patch of Sunshine* sold will be donated in Ed's name toward cancer research, with the hope that, in the future, others may avoid the end that Ed faced.

People handle grief in different ways. I stopped writing my current novel and turned to poetry, churning out poems at a feverish pace. I wrote without censoring or filtering anything. Realizing Ed's birthday was approaching, I had a target date and wrote toward it.

In early March, I handed my poems over to Samia Perkins to whom I owe a debt of gratitude. Aware of my self-imposed, insane deadline, Sami read my entire collection over the course of a weekend. She served as my editor and touchstone for this project, providing invaluable feedback. The collection is better because of her input.

I would also like to acknowledge and thank Catherine Jeu for helping me with cover advice. Having an artist of her caliber call my childlike artwork and cover printing "charming" meant the world to me—and made me brave enough to put it out there for the world, even though, clearly, my talent is better suited for words.

A Patch of Sunshine is thematically divided into seven parts. Part 1 contains love poems I had written before Ed's death. Part 3 contains haikus that are fairly evenly divided between before and after (other haikus are sprinkled thematically throughout the book). Parts 2, 4, 5 and 6 are poems inspired by Ed and infused with his spirit. His memory made family history seem more important to me, so Part 2 contains true family stories put into poetry. Part 4 deals with the uncomfortable topics of death, grieving, aging. Part 5 provides lighter fare that balances the darkness in part 4. If these were

Jeopardy categories, Part 6 would be Potpourri. Lastly, because I was feeling melancholy and nostalgic, I chose to add poems (and lyrics) I wrote last century. Even though the date range I provide extends from 1973-1996, the bulk of Part 7 dates from '79-'86, with only two exceptions: one that I wrote ten years after that and one that I wrote a few months shy of my thirteenth birthday. I included this latter one not only because it started me on a journey as a writer but because I feel it captures perfectly the essence of Ed. So I chose to conclude this book with that poem.

Ultimately, I hope that I've done Ed proud and that this book serves as a worthy homage to him. If this work falls short of expectations, the failing is mine. I would like to think Ed would have loved this collection and that somewhere he is smiling. Ed brought more than a patch of sunshine into the lives of all he touched.

Prologue

I've sung the song of "Sunshine"

Sensing Sunshine

Sometimes I've seen the sunshine
as a veil through forest trees.
I've smelled its fragrance, so fine,
wafting on a morning breeze.

I've felt the burn of its heat
when I've laid out in excess.
I've heard its sound of retreat
as it settled in the west.

I've sung the song of "Sunshine"
when the eastern sky I faced
blossomed in colors divine.
Oh, Sunshine! I love your taste.

Part 1

One extra dollop of attention

(Love Poems)

Doors

Do I dare open doors
that, once opened, can't be closed?
I chart a dangerous course,
there's so much for me to lose.

But if this door stays shuttered
with my feelings locked inside,
a part of me just shudders
at the coward who would hide

and deny any potential
of a flame bursting from a spark.
For me, then, it's essential
to push this heavy door ajar.

Kisses

My lips meet your lips.
Gentle, slow, sweet caress.
As first kisses often are.
My lips meet your lips.
Urgent, searching, insistent.
A prelude to something more.
My lips meet your lips.
Hot and strong, persistent.
The afterglow that long endures.
My lips meet yours
and never want to leave.

5 a.m.

You're the first person on my mind today
You're the first person on my mind
That doesn't leave me much more to say
You're the first person all the time

Math (of Love)

Two souls intersecting,
existing on one plane,
geometrically aligned,
exponentially refined,
willing to defy all odds
just to be together.

Force (of Love)

Love is the greatest force existing in our universe.
Nothing is more binding, more accepting, or more diverse.
Procreation, creativity: both children of love.
Imagination, ingenuity: by-products of.
Love motivates, anticipates, the actions that we take.
Love generates, accelerates, the feelings that we make.
Love devastates, decapitates, asunder and apart
Nothing else but love has power to break a human heart.

Velocity (of Love)

$E=mc^2$. Somehow that defines the speed of light.
Love is faster. Love is instantaneous, spontaneous.
Love is ageless, timeless. Love is everywhere and all at once.
Love travels beyond all confines at the velocity of now.

Everything My Heart Desires

I want chocolate in the moonlight—and love
I want ice cream after midnight—and love
I want everything a man can gain
A house, a fortune, acclaim and fame,
A reputation for success
My share, or more, of happiness
Yes, all of this; yet, all of this
I'd trade away and never miss—for love.

Wordless

Your eyes tease,
but not nearly so much
as your tongue.

A Leap Worth Taking

I find the girl exciting
I wonder
if I excite her

I know she loves my writing
I want her
to love the writer

It's not that big a leap to take.
The hand that crafts the words she loves
is guided by one man. This man.

I want her
to see this man
as worthy of her love

I want her
to understand
she'd always be enough

I want her
plain and simple
I want her

Parallel Universes

We walk and talk about Oprah,
my novel, life, motivation.
You are animated, passionate,
deserving of my admiration.
At one point, you say words so touching
That I want to hold you and kiss you.

I think about parallel universes...

If there are an infinite number of me's
Walking with an infinite number of you's
In this precise moment,
In this exact circumstance,
Repeated to infinity,
I am sure I must have kissed you in at least fifty-three.

But I only care about this one universe...

And what happens within each now.
I wish I could channel that bolder me
From one of those other fifty-three
And hold you tight and kiss you long.
I want you to look into my eyes and see
limitless possibilities, unparalleled love.

Unshareable

Emotions held in check to keep my heart from reeling.
I've shared everything with you except my deepest feelings.
Time is of the essence: treat love like a perishable.
If guarded feelings block romance, I'm unshareable.

Unraveling Like a Bad Movie

The words won't come.
The uncomfortable silence
sits between us
like an unwelcomed guest,
creating a chasm
of Grand Canyon proportions,
belying my ability
to reach out and hold your hand
if I so chose.
But, of course,
I don't.

Chinese-Water-Torture Love

Drip.
Drip.
Drip.
Drop. Drop.
One look.
One touch.
One smile.
One hug.
One extra dollop of attention.
One simple act of pure affection.
One subtle word of adoration.
It's too late now to make this stop.
Drip-drop.
Drip-drop.
Drip-drop. Drop. Drop.
Little by little, 'til all at once
I am the one drowning.

Sidewalk Artwork

Sidewalk artwork made in chalk
is not a medium for the faint of heart.
It's time-consuming to create this art.
We walked among the chalk work,
admiring the artistry.
A light rain fell, blurring images.
Then a hard rain washed them
completely away.

Two weeks later, our relationship
also ended in a rain of tears
that smeared your make-up
like sidewalk artwork made in chalk.

Signs

I look for signs we're more than friends
I search for clues and evidence
of togetherness, love and bliss.

I do my chart of pros and cons
And know deep down that my heart longs
To sing a song of love like this.

The first time that I'd dared touch you
I felt your body tense and knew
We each were at a different place.

Months later, you hugged me. I felt
Your entire body melt
Into my arms for that embrace.

That moment replays in my mind.
It seems to me a hopeful sign.

The Great Divide

Cat gave me a formula: half my age
plus seven. You pooh-poohed that in a rage
even though (I hope not because) you fit.
I, too, found this formula a bit
too arbitrary. It doesn't ring true.
Still, it gave me hope I had a chance with you.

Megan told me age does not factor in
the equation. It's up to the woman
to decide if the difference is worth
the effort. Happiness is rare on earth.
Finding it is the only real factor.
Being with that soul is all that matters.

It's pretty clear where I stand on this:
Life, liberty, pursuit of happiness.
You alone decide if the gap is too wide,
or if your heart rides across the divide.
My emotions aside, I'm on the wrong side.

Poetry Sublime

Poems are like paintings
meant to be admired
one at a time
savored like fine wine.

Poems are like sunsets
unique and glorious
yes, ordinary
but extraordinary

Poems are like nothing else
when poetry's sublime
I can't let it go unsaid
You're the best I've ever read

Deep Questions

You ask me complex questions and I give you simple answers.
"What are your thoughts on God?" you ask and I say,
        "Either God exists
or God is a concept." There have been times in my life
when I've been in both camps. I only know that I do not know.
You ask me if I believe in soul mates and I scoff, "No."

I am reminded of another day when we walked together
down Santana Row. My mind numbed by pain meds, the exact
question eludes me, but it might as well have been
"What is the meaning of life?" Perhaps emboldened by the
        drugs,
I put my arm around you and said, "This. This is all that
        matters."

I meant it then with all my heart, and mean it still. Yet,
        now, you ask
the unfairest question of all. Do I believe in soul mates?
You ask me complex questions and I give you simple answers.
What I believe does not matter. I could be wrong. I only know
that if I did believe in soul mates, mine sits across the table.

Addiction

I want you to know
If I overdose on love
It will be your fault

Part 2

So many mouths to feed that year

(Family stories put to verse)

The Cloak of History

Family stories
handed down make the fabric
from which we are cut

The Great Escape

In 1933, Hitler, whom my mom's dad already disliked,
decreed that universities could not have Jewish professors.
Being a professor himself, my grandfather had friends
in the faculty who were Jewish and he saw this as an affront.
Perhaps he realized worse things were on the horizon
—perhaps I give him too much credit—
but whatever his reasons, he chose to flee Germany illegally.

He taught French and English at a German university
—and he spoke all three languages fluently. Relying on
        that skill,
he dressed as a French monsignor and boarded a train.
A German soldier asked him for his papers as he attempted
to exit at the first stop in France. My grandfather feigned
a lack of understanding, answering only in flawless French.

Perhaps there wasn't yet a strict adherence to rules
—perhaps the soldier was exasperated by the language
        barrier—
but whatever the reason—luck, timing, the hand of God—
my grandfather was allowed off the train without papers.
Shortly thereafter he came to America, completing his escape.

Hungry Henry

As a young girl, my mom
watched her Aunt Luella
pack six sandwiches everyday
for Uncle Henry's lunch.

"Does he eat them all?" she asked, wide-eyed
to which her aunt quickly replied,
"Oh, yes! Henry's hungry.
He works up quite the appetite."

My mom learned the truth years later.
But when she was young, with the war just ended
and the Great Depression still a recent reminder,
Henry had five hungry co-workers
who otherwise would have gone without.

My Father's First Car

At 18, my dad ran his parents' deli one summer
with the promise of a first car as a reward.
In the fall, Dad perpetually pestered his dad,
who was slow on delivering upon that promise.

Grandpa was out gardening when Dad again approached.
Dirt on his hands, dirt on his pants, Grandpa stood up,
and said, "All right. Let's go now." He wiped his hands
upon his overalls, and together they immediately left.

They went to the Chevrolet lot to pick a fine, affordable car.
Grandpa, in his sweat soaked tee shirt and grass stained
overalls, looked more a hillbilly than a serious customer.
Every salesman on the lot, the whole lot of them, ignored him.

Steaming, Grandpa said, "Come on, we're going there."
Dad was ready to complain—until he saw where there was—
Grandpa pointed across the street to the Hudson dealership.
Hudsons, pure luxury, were far more expensive than Chevies.

The Hudson salesmen were much less willing to prejudge
a man standing on their lot and much more willing to deal.
The deal struck, Grandpa—never one to leave well enough
        alone—
paraded Dad back to the Chevy dealer and asked for the
        manager.

"I came to buy a Chevy, and you lost my business," he said.
Grandpa shoved his Hudson bill of sale—cash, fully paid—
and berated the man for running a sales staff that would fail
to help a cash-carrying customer. Their loss was Dad's gain.

Grandpa stormed off the lot, undoubtedly pleased with
        himself,
but not nearly as pleased as Dad, the owner of a new 1950
        Hudson.

Never Again

Grandma Jean—my dad's mom—was hit by a truck
She was told never again would she walk.

After weeks of care, she left in a wheel chair.
Her sons carried her and it up the stairs.

It was a struggle for them to reach the top
When they did, Grandma had had enough

She stood up and pushed the chair back down,
Crashing, smashing, it fell to the ground.

"Never again," she said, "will I use that."
Then she turned and walked into their flat.

Vonnie's Husband

When Mom's grandmother was 96
she moved into a rest home about 20 minutes
from where my parents lived.

Dad, whom she called "Vonnie's husband,"
would visit her nearly every day. Mom
(Vonnie only to her side of the family; Yvonne
to everyone else, including my dad) would visit
about once a week.
One of the first things

Great grandma complained about was
"All the old people" she was surrounded by.
"They don't care about nothing," she said.
"I like to read the newspaper everyday
to keep up with things."
Oh, and could she!

She knew the names of all of her grandchildren
and great grandchildren. She had 12 kids herself,
so the offspring of her offspring and the offspring of theirs
numbered very near 100. Yet, she could rattle off the names
of the branches from her tree like nobody's business.

When she had lived in this rest home for about two years,
seeing Dad nearly every day and Mom about once a week,
a strange thing happened: no longer was Dad
"Vonnie's husband." Great grandma call him "Walt"
and my mom, her granddaughter, became "Walt's wife."

Potatoes

When my dad Walt was a small lad
He and his brothers would go
By the railroad tracks and wait
For the train to chug-a-lug by them.

The point was food. Potatoes fell.
And Lou, Paul, Walt, and Richie
Would collect them as if each
Spud was as valuable as gold.

Home they'd march, their pockets full
and soon their stomachs would be, too.
Their mother made potato soup
—for breakfast, potato pancakes.

So many mouths to feed that year
and only fear itself to fear.

Carrots

I surreptitiously walked to my girlfriend's house
back in the eighth grade. It was the spring of '74;
the place, Miami, Arizona. Her name was Judy
and she was a freckled, blue-eyed beauty
who easily stole my heart, even before she passed
me a love note I kept for years afterwards.

I'm sure someone knew about my near-daily trip
to see my first love, but, fortunately, no one
ever called me out on it. On one visit, Judy
offered me a carrot—I'm being literal,
and talking about the vegetable, not some
dangling reward. She had two carrots.

One was exactly the kind of carrot I love:
slender and sweet; delicious to eat.
The other was a thick beast of a thing
too hard to bite and too bitter to the taste.
Of course, it was this latter one she offered me.
I ate it, but I was envious watching hers devoured.

Being smarter at love than me, Judy sensed
something amiss and asked me pointblank.
The petulant adolescent me told her exactly
what the problem was. She listened. Then she
said, "I gave you the thick carrot because that's
the kind I like best." I felt two inches small.

Looking back, now, I realize I learned
Everything I needed to know about love
from a carrot. Put other's first. It's a good
lesson and I'm glad I learned it at thirteen.

Beets

I tend to be an even keeled kind of guy.
I'm not one to lose my temper. So the one time
I blew my stack is ingrained in our family lore,
so much so that I have to endure the oft-repeated
phrase, "don't feed John beets."
And while I'm not proud of the beet incident, as it is
known by its witnesses, it was never about beets.

The beet incident occurred after my freshmen year
of college. I had spent a whole glorious year living
by my own rules—lax as they were—and, suddenly,
I'm back home for the summer, treated like a child again.
Worse, home wasn't home. My family moved my freshmen
year, so the "home" I returned to was not the home I had
departed from. I knew no one. Saw none of my friends.

I was miserable—the worst kind of teen-aged angst kind
of miserable—the kind without end—the kind that needs
to be inflicted upon others, so they, too, can feel your pain.
My mom exacerbated the pain at every opinion I held
that differed from that of little boy me—and Mom had no
problem saying, "You didn't use to feel that way when you
were little." The fuse lit at the beginning of summer

neared its payload. The explosion was sudden—insanely,
wildly, (and in retrospect only) comically out of proportion.
Mom served what I'm sure was a wonderful salad, but
it was topped by beets—something she knew little boy me
        hated.
I turned beet red and yelled at the top of my vocal range
—from a place I didn't know existed, "Beets!
You know I hate beets! Why did you give me beets!"

and other such nonsensical tidbits regarding beets.
When my tirade finally ended, my mom said, "All right.
I won't serve you beets." And no one from my family has since.
The odd thing is, probably even then, I'll eat beets.
I kind of like them, in fact. The thing is, sometimes
it's not about the beets, even if beets is in every sentence.
Sometimes the beets are served metaphorically.

Trish Gets Her Wish

With apologies to my sister Trish,
who tells this story better than I...
By the time Trish was a teen-ager,
Mom had four teens and a 3-year-old to handle.
It made for a harried, hectic schedule.

As Trish and Mom left the house for the grocery store,
Trish, as was her wont, joked, "Can I drive?"
To her surprise, Mom said, "Sure" and handed her
the keys. Halfway to their destination, Mom turned
and looked at Trish. "Do you have your driver's license?"
"No," Trish answered. "Then why are you driving?" asked
     Mom.
Without missing a beat, Trish replied, "Because you said I
     could."

Mom's ZZ Top Top

Mom had a yellow tee shirt
colorfully emblazoned with ZZ Top.
She loved her ZZ Top top.
She wore it at home.
She wore it in public.
She wore it pretty much everywhere
except to church.

One day, while watching television,
Mom saw ZZ Top perform.
Horrified, she liked neither
their music nor their look.
Her favorite shirt lost its standing,
never to be worn again.

When I asked her about it,
she replied—as only Mom can
when she's the last to know
something everyone else long knew—
completely deadpanned,
"I thought ZZ Top
was a brand, not a band."

Part 3

Applause from the sky

(Haikus)

Poetry Barker

Get your haikus here!
Each one its own adventure.
Dive in and get lost.

BBQ

A full rack of ribs
Slathered in a spicy sauce
I'm in hog heaven!

Workday Blues

Six o'clock alarm
Shatters the silence of sleep
Dreams interrupted

Big Bang

Major explosion
Existence from nothingness
Everything now is

Creationism

A snap of fingers
Existence from nothingness
I am who I am

Our Universe

Chaos and violence
Disorderly chunks of mass
Move blazingly fast

Earth

A small speck of blue
In a sea of silent black
Supports me and you

Lake and Rock

Mirror of water
Splintered by a skipping stone
Settles placidly

Time and Tide

Rising tides come in
Destroy castles made of sand
The sea wins again

Thunderclap

Lightning strikes the earth
Drowning the patter of rain
Applause from the sky

Sunshine

A patch of sunshine
Glimmers through the windowpane
A cat stakes its claim

#16 Dream

Create wildly
Dare to do what others don't
The heart of earth: art

Fallacy #3

Making a living
while good, should not be confused
with making a life.

Trust

Hard earned over time
Once broken forever lost
Like a wedding vow

Selfie

an Ego driven
photo opportunity
always in arm's reach

Lord of the Ring Trilogy

Frodo keeps it safe
the Fellowship protects him
until good prevails

*The Pompous Arrogance Prevalent in Thinking an
Epic Saga can be Reduced to a Haiku*

A trilogy stripped
its bare essence thus exposed
becomes far grander

Styx and Stones

Rock and roll dreamers
who come sail away with me
find satisfaction

Still Art

Poets paint with words
Their black and white canvasses
Shaded with meaning

Screenplay

Painting a story
To spark imaginations
Using sight and sound

Novel

Expansive free verse
Where rules are meant to be broken
Unconfined by form

First Drafts

Vomit on the page
Mocking your ability
Screams for a clean up

Unfinished Business

Half-finished poems
like stacks of dirty laundry
demand attending

Lifelong Joy

Shouldering sunshine,
John Denver made me smile
Long ago—and now

Success

Choose the life you live
Give it all you've got to give
Love with all your heart

Beautiful Music

Some people write songs
Others prefer to right wrongs
I want to hear both

Part 4

What happened to the little boy?

(Poems of Time, Life, and Death)

Photograph

I used to hold you
in my arms
Now I hold you
in my wallet
You're safe
a living memory
But I preferred you
Living

New Life

Dead leaves—grounded, stripped
from branches that were home,
discarded like coffee grounds—
collected with care,
lovingly pressed
between pages
of a photo album,
their beauty
to live on.

Room to Grow

floating, floating
darkness
fluid
a constant, soothing heartbeat
—pa-pum, pa-pum—
muffled sounds
the rush of blood
the constant, rhythmic drum
—pa-pum, pa-pum, pa-pum—
a push, a shove, a labor of love
blinding light
a rush of new sounds
—but the absence of the comforting pounds—
sudden fear
a scream and tears

Memories

Memories are not infallible,
repeatable or deletable.
Some memories are as nebulous
as a nebula. Difficult to grab
from thin air. Fleeting wisps of thought
that wander away as we move
from one room to the next
and wonder what we came there for.

Sometimes they are black holes in our minds.
Remind me, again, how we know each other—
"oh, that's right" though we don't really recall.
Some memories are visual, emotional, dreamlike
fragments, speeding around our mind like a comet.
They are things we want to hold dearly
because sometimes memory is all that lives on
and it is the most important thing, therefore.

Childhood Recaptured

What happened to the little boy
who saw whimsy in clouds, faces
on mountain edges, adventure
with each new day? What happened
to the boy who heard music
floating on the wind, dancing
off the ocean, running through the fields?

Growing up does not justify the lack of joy
now existing in all the places
that held such wonder for the boy.
At least, it shouldn't. Deep down
I am still that boy. I remember
the adventure of life and long
to live that way again.

100 Birthdays

I would rather be old and wrinkly,
attempting to blow out 100 candles
atop my birthday cake than to contemplate
never seeing another sunrise.

The Stranger

Who is this man I see looking back at me
from my bathroom mirror each morning?
He looks nothing like I picture myself.
When I take the time to do so, I am young
and vital. And I think and act as though I am.
It is only through the reactions and interactions
I have with those who are currently young and vital
that I realize they see the stranger
who stares at me from my mirror.
They don't see me at all.

State of Mind

I never felt old a day in my life
Then you died
I haven't felt young since

Ageism

An -ism isn't necessarily bad, but as far
as –isms go, ageism is the nearest
I've experienced to prejudice of any kind.
I have been blind (or have tried to be)
to race, gender, religion—things
that attempt to divide. I never realized
age was one of those things.
                              Then I got old.

87

Four score and seven years
would make a decent lifespan;
yet in the grander scheme,
it is a mere drop in the cosmic
time bucket, barely negligible.

How important we like to think we are
on our small planet near our small star,
a speck in the vastness of infinity.

Dust to Dust

All of us are stardust.
From a violent death
of exploding matter,
the substance of stars sent
outward in space in an attempt
to live on in another form

finds itself in us, when we are born.
Each of us stars, full of potential.
In death, our souls exploding
outward from the shell in an attempt
to live on in another form,

we return to that cosmic circle of life
that none of us fully comprehend.

Eileen

Because I couldn't do you justice with a poem
I wrote you a whole novel, lyric and poetic.
Knowing you'll never read it, the novel really was for me
to assuage the guilt over—and to come to terms with—not
            knowing
How could I not know?

I missed your funeral
because I did not know.

The day I learned of your death
—news three months overdue—
I curled into the fetal position
and cried all day,
too stunned, too shocked.
Speechless.

My love didn't do you justice when you were living;
yet, I always thought I would have the chance to set things
            right.
How could I know you'd leave this earthly plane at 30?

Guilt and grief—two ugly beasts—
fed upon the sadness and the loss.
And stayed.
Years, they stayed. Years!
Years you didn't get to see.

It seems like yesterday
I held you in my arms
and kissed you gently.

How I wish I could today.

Eulogy

Once, you told me you had practiced giving mine
and—while I'm sure you said wonderful things
about the kind of man I was when I was alive
—being that I am still among the living, I found
the concept both disturbing and disconcerting.
In retrospect, you would have had words at the ready.
Being something I did not once rehearse
I was unprepared to give yours.

Unknown Territory

I am in no hurry
to learn the great unknown
to cross that final threshold.
After all, it may only be an ending
when I so wanted a beginning.
Don't spoil the end for me—
I'll enjoy the journey.
I am in no hurry.

Normal

Everyone says things will return to normal.
I don't know what normal is anymore
—or if it even existed before—
but how could anything be normal if you
are not part of it? Everyone is wrong.
There's a deep hole a million miles long
that no amount of normal can ever fill.

The Greatness of Ed

There are no words
—I've tried so hard
to set the record straight.

Ed was awesome,
plain and simple.
Put plainly, Ed was simply great.

There are no words
—I've cried so hard
Words dried up, tears speak loudly.

It tears my soul
my sole purport
Writing—words I wrote so proudly

Now fall so short.
Now fail to say
The truth that needs to be said

I wish I knew
how to convey
the greatness of my dear friend Ed.

In Absentia

The path was here not long ago.
I stepped firmly upon it,
confident in my action.
A phone call changed my direction.
A plane flight diverted my intention.
A tragic loss demanded my attention,
obscured the path completely.
I know it was here not long ago.
My steps uncertain, I am so
Lost.

Grief

I lost my best friend
Ashes scattered to the wind
Memory remains

Hide and Seek

"...seven, eight, nine, ten.
Ready or not, here I come!"
Mere child's play for death.

Death

For the same reason
I seek out younger women
You shun older men

Valentine Vases

Morbid thoughts have I
to see only metaphor
as red roses die

The Crime of Wasting Time

It's the stuff of life
Fairly allotted each day
But days are numbered

Part 5

Gurgle, gurgle, burp, burp, gurple

(Poems with humorous intent)

Political Animus

Capitol business
Where donkeys and elephants
Fight like cats and dogs

A Nation Divided

It has been argued that Democrats and Republicans
just cannot get along. That conservatism and liberalism
are polar opposites. Each side thinks the other Fascist.
It's easy to understand the vitriolic in the political:
conservatives are fiercely patriotic,
Staunch defenders of the Constitution,
and strong believers in personal rights and freedom.
Liberals, on the other hand, are strong believers in personal
        rights and freedom,
Staunch defenders of the Constitution,
and fiercely patriotic.
Two such conflicting viewpoints can rarely see eye to eye.

Big Fish

One state
Two state
Red state
Blue state

Mix a little here
Fix a little there
Mix, mix, mix
Fix, fix, fix
Oh, these messy politics!

Add some red to the melting pot
Add some blue and see what we've got
Gurgle, gurgle, burp, burp, gurple
Look! All 50 states are purple!

Every issue now resolved!
Every problem neatly solved!
We can all go call a truce
Thanks, in part, to Dr. Seuss.

FAQ

All questions answered
What is the meaning of life?
Let me Google that

Mid-Life Crisis

My two friends won't admit this phase
has hit them hard in many ways.
Each has made his mid-life blunder.
Will I make mine? I often wonder.

I chuckle as I drive my Porsche
(the one I bought since my divorce
after my wife's discovering
my fling with that 20-something).

How could each friend not see his error?
At least I know I'm self-aware.

Rambling Treadmill Thoughts

I download my heart health app
And upload my Fitbit shit
I exercise on a computerized machine
while streaming Netflix
and watching hot chicks
coated with a sexy sheen
that hardly convinces me
they are putting in any real effort.
Sort of like how my ex-girlfriend, Jean
treated our relationship,
but that's a story best left untold.
If I dwell on her I'll have to come clean
And that will make me angry and if I get angry,
I work out harder and if I work out too hard,
I might forget to check out the girls who are sexy and lean.
And that defeats the whole purpose of going to the gym,
      know what I mean?

Jokes

Did you hear this one
A man walks into a bar
And forgets to drink

Puns

Dogwood without leaves
Is like a toothless smile
But beware its bark

A Glaring Example

English is colorful, but flawed.
When something is important to us,
we can be quite inventive.
For example, take women's breasts.
They go by several nicknames
(you can decide which you like best):

Headlights, hooters, honkers,
Pillows, airbags, knockers,
Milkshakes and cupcakes,
Cha-chas and tatas,
Torpedoes and mosquito bites
(depending, clearly, on their size),
Tomatoes, peaches, cantaloupes, melons,
Cans, jugs, rack (usually with "nice")
The girls, the twins, bombs and boobs

I've scratched the surface but that's enough
To make this point: for all the different ways
we use it, we have only one word for love.
Shouldn't love be so important we'd have a variety
of words differentiating its meanings? I mean,
we use love in a hundred ways:
I love ice cream, daydreams,
my mother and father,
my brother and daughter,
football and baseball bats,
beaches, weekends, dogs and cats,
fine wine, good food, and life
and, of course, my lovely wife.
Yet, somehow, the one word
is supposed to suffice?
You'd think we'd have at least a pair.

Breaking Down Poetry for the Uninitiated

Foot meter line
Imagery and images (optional rhyme)
Stanza

Punctuation (also optional: notice missing commas above
    and below)
Allusion allegory alliteration (none, some, or all—in
    moderation)
Simile metaphor theme wordplay (one or more
    recommended)

Twist!
Art (debatable)

Attack of the Zones

An end zone is for scoring
The erogenous zone is for exploring
Neither happens if stuck in the worst zone

Put me in a Blue Zone or a Red Zone
the Green Zone or a Dead Zone,
or Chernobyl's Exclusion Zone.
I'll even choose the ozone,
Any zone, please, but the friend zone.

Online Ideal

On LinkedIn, I am professional, capable, accomplished
      and my profile is 95% complete
On eHarmony, I sound energetic, enjoyable and wildly
      sociable
On Facebook, I have 4000 friends and my timeline never ends
On Twitter, you can read my tweets from Monday to mundane
On Instagram, I post photos galore of all the fun I want
      you to think I have on a regular basis
On Spotify, I'm a hip and cool trend setter with tons of
      followers listening to my picks
Yep, I'm a pretty happening guy online. Ideal, you might say.
Too bad reality gets in the way.

The Meaning of Life Succinctly Explained in
Seventeen Syllables

Those who seek meaning
From random absurdity
Must have OCD

Part 6

With hopes to be immortalized

(Poems of various themes)

Blank Page

I stare intently
Thinking grandiose thoughts I can't convey on paper
Searching for the right word,
a task as difficult—or more so
—as finding that proverbial needle in a haystack
The blank screen daunting,
taunting me, haunting me
A never-ending circle of futility
I wait for the screen to fill itself
as if by magic
with perfect prose
—yet it never does
It stays blank
no matter how long
I stare intently

Rejection

I have often joked that dating
in high school and college
prepared me for a life as a writer:
rejection, rejection, rejection.

While it usually gets a laugh,
the truth is, it's not funny.
You have to have a pretty thick skin
to handle the kind of rejection

that is so easily heaped upon
a labor of love. Some children
are only loved by their parents,
but it's hard, as the parent

not to appreciate the errant
as well as the honest. Perhaps,
the child will be loved by someone,
someone desperately in need

of exactly what the child
provides. It's that kind of thinking
that makes me carry on, and say,
"Hear me now"—and know that I am here.

Procrastination

It's amazing how much can get done in five minutes.
It's equally amazing how much time we'll spend
avoiding a task that takes mere minutes.
The effort of avoidance is greater than the effort
needed to complete the task. What's with this self-inflicted
anxiety? Why the willful postponement
of even the simplest things? We would be much
happier creatures if we just learned to act now.

Michelle Pfeiffer

Many years ago, I saw Michelle Pfeiffer
riding a bicycle in Dana Point.
At first, I didn't know it was her.
As I stared at the approaching figure,
my mind struggled to recollect how I knew her
—because, of course, I did—

and when realization and recognition hit me,
she saw it in my face and smiled coyly.
And, just as fast, she had passed me,
leaving me to turn in her wake,
wanting to say something–though I didn't know her
—because, of course, I didn't—

a forgettable moment in a lifetime
of similar encounters for her;
yet, indelibly etched in my mind.
For the briefest of instances,
celebrity and I shared the same plane of existence
— because, of course, we all do—

and, for the record, Michelle Pfeiffer
was even more beautiful in real life
—because, of course, we all are—

American Dreaming

You can ask my ma
You can ask my pa
I've been working hard
Down in Omaha

Met a girl named Dawn
We've got it going on
Think I'll marry her
Before the summer's gone

We'll make a comfy home
of our very own
there ain't nobody
wants to live alone

We'll plant a little tree
Make a family
With three or four kids
If it's up to me

Down in Omaha
We'll be standing tall
Living out the dream
Yeah, we got it all

Hurricane

My mama told me that I'm insane
I'm out dancing with the Hurricane.
It's the single greatest adrenaline rush
tangled, torn, and twisted in Katrina's clutch.
In her windswept whirl with my hair unkempt,
every ounce of energy in me spent,
I'm already ready to repeat the pain.
Damn, girl! You sure have an apt nickname.

Cat and Mouse

My friend Cat has a dog named Mouse
Cat's dog Mouse has full run of her house
When Cat walks Mouse no one finds it odd
They just see a woman out walking her dog

The cat and mouse games that Cat and Mouse play
Are filled with joy and can last all day
I get a chuckle and so does Cat's spouse
to think they have neither a cat nor a mouse.

Queen of Hearts

The hand is dealt. I spy a pair of queens.
I raise. Three callers come along for the ride.
The flop is sweet: the queen of hearts! I check
and call a pot-sized bet. So does the man
to my left. Three watch the turn. A danger card.
The jack of hearts. So many draws. With bold
aggression, I deny pot odds and push.
"I'm all-in." "Call." The river holds my fate.

Poker

I look at rockets
then at the early raiser
I three bet all-in

River Bet

I sit with the nuts
Teen-age girl monologue plays
Call me, please call me

Advice for Playing Tight

Wait for better hands
Keep a stoic countenance
Mix in bluffs and traps

Advice for Playing Loose

Play aggressively
Bet and raise to rake in chips
Fold to resistance

Hope Springs Eternal

Every year at springtime
Giants of the diamond appear
to hone their craft
with glove and bat
with hopes to be immortalized
as the last team standing
come the fall

Observe the Acrobat

Observe the acrobat:
She moves with graceful ease.
Her leaps and spins, midair
—as if from a trapeze —
exhibit *savoir faire*,
make the difficult a breeze.
Her muscular debonair
shows artful expertise.
Observe the acrobat:
My awe-inspiring cat.

Line

A panicked admission by a cast member on the stage
A hopeful casting of bait to secure today's catch
A tired cliché used to catch women in a bar
A barring division beyond which one is not free to cross
The point on the basketball court from which free throws
       are shot
Point A to point B at one hundred eighty degrees
Waiting behind one hundred eighty people at the DMV
But wait! My favorite is a good verse of poetry

One Liner

Can a poem be just one line? Why not?

Poverty

Kneading bread
beats needing bread.
We take for granted
grocery stores
constantly stocked with variety.
More than we could ever eat
in a year on display every day
while others beg for their daily bread.

What Would Jesus Do?

I hear this question asked.
I am more interested in the answer.
Even more so in the action.

Do as Jesus would do
is far better than intellectualizing
an answer to a hypothetical question.

But, then, that gets us back to the golden rule,
doesn't it? Do unto others
as you would have them do unto you.

That's what Jesus would do
and it seems a goodly way of living.

In the Eyes of God

If we were, all of us, flawless
Love would be narcissistic

And we would, each of us, be gods
Instead of created in His image

But just because we have flaws
doesn't mean we aren't perfect

Part 7

Beyond the barriers of time

(Poems and lyrics from 1973-1996)

A Lover's Gaze

There's a fire burning brightly,
There's a shooting star ablaze—
So don't you take it lightly
When you see two lovers gaze.

There's a certain kind of something
In the eyes of those who stare
So intently into nothing
And yet see something there.

Now I may be a romantic
To say that love cures all,
But believe me I was frantic
When it came my turn to fall.

Now maybe it hurts a little
And maybe quite a bit,
But somewhere in the middle
You'll find the perfect fit

That says this love is right for you
And says this love will last.
And like that shooting star that flew
You'll find it happened fast.

Something Simple

Friends told me to write about something simple:
Write about her eyes, or smile, or dimple,
or hair they advised, but don't give everything
away at once or so easily. I think
they have a valid point; but my problem
is how to take her eyes, say, and not rob them
of their beauty by reducing them to words.
For words—once written, read or spoken, heard—
do not translate into the visual
image that the eye with one casual
glance registers. And the beauty the eye
beholds is a beauty that does not lie
like words. Words lie on the page without malice
until read. The trick with words is to balance
The beautiful eye and the banal pimple
and make this complex balance sound so simple.

Frozen Image

I see myself reflected in the pond
still frozen with the winter ice. It melts,
cascading to the spring, the river next,
the ocean last. Waves toss the aqua sky
some salty summer spray so thirsty clouds
may drink until they burst. Rains fall. Lakes swell.
My image mirrored on sheets of winter glass.
Icy myself, I melt into the spring.

On Writing Uninspired Poetry

A line is difficult to write.
More so when words come late at night
And days were spent with a constant (though
A shifting) image. It's very tough—
Believe you me—to write a concrete
And striking piece. So great a feat
Is still accomplished every time
A poet needs to speak his mind,
But has nothing to say. That said,
I rest my pen and head for bed.

Pieces (of the Whole)

Sunshine, seaside, raindrops, ocean tides,
Full moons, starlight, blue skies, summer nights.
Spring days, winter snow, fresh air, autumn glow,
Clear lakes, a fragrant rose, green hills, running does.
Morning dew, waterfalls, redwood trees;
All of these, and more than these all: you

Picture Perfect

Is love this and no more? I hope for more, but
My hopes always remain unanswered. Still, I
Can dream dreams of a time when love will be—not
A trap set by a huntress shooting soft sighs
Through my mind but—a freedom felt by those caught
With free will. A will freed by powers inside
The mind. Love is all this and more. But what need
For each other do we fulfill? We both see

That our love, what we have as love, is not whole
Like freed love; what we love is being in love.
Can appearance be picture perfect when all
It is is just appearance? Love is too tough
To maintain. I have thought about it: our fall
In love; springing from depths—to nothing more. Love!
In our never ending search for perfection
Do you think love was ever our intention?

Diverging from the Core

Beyond the barriers of time,
Flesh is naught. But thoughts on thought grow
Like rivers, running. Through my mind

A million thoughts become entwined,
Millions. Pregnant notions hallowed
Beyond the barriers. Of time

We know so little. Of love we find
Much less. Sex is sought—our lust pools
Like rivers running through. My mind

Imagines fantasies of the carnal kind,
Penetrates these thoughts, but cannot go
Beyond. The barriers of time

Imprison us in flesh, resigned.
Time is cruel; it twists our marrow
Like rivers. Running through my mind

This inspiration seems divine:
Time is not. To think, my thought flows
Beyond the barriers of time
Like rivers running through my mind.

Beautiful You

Angel of lightness dressed in your faded blue jeans
One look in your brown eyes have fulfilled my gold starlit
      dreams
You're an ethereal sunbeam that lights up my sky
A fiery comet that burns through my night
And I've never felt so alive

And all that I know
is all that I knew
And all I can think of is
Beautiful You

Rainbows of colors shine through the silver streaked clouds
Your hand brushes my cheek, eliminates all of my doubts
You are substance and style all wrapped up in grace
You are softness of spirit in every embrace
And I've never been so amazed

You're beautiful, so beautiful
All I can think of is
Beautiful You.

Lessons of Love and Lust in Four Parts

Part I: Lisa
I'd be in heaven to have her whole
For half of her love I would give my soul
A quarter of her love would be enough for me
But to tell you quite honestly
I'd settle for a fifth of Lisa

Funny thing she may not be the kind of woman for me

Part II: Terry
He's got Terry and I'm so very
Disappointed with life
He's got Terry the kind of girl I'd marry
An impractical wife

Terry, oh, Terry
Oh, why did you tear me
Apart at the seams?
Terry, oh, Terry
Oh, you could have spared me
My heart and my dreams

Part III: Randi
Randi was what all the guys would call stacked
There wasn't one physical point that she lacked
She was probably a nine, but to me she's a ten
For a while she was mine, how I wish she were again

All this fuss about a girl named Randi
Her hot and slow kisses were sweeter than candy
And, oh, those places that she could send me
I never met anyone else like her

Part IV: A Different Lisa

Lisa, I love you.
Now tell me is that such a crime?
Lisa, I want you.
Maybe even 'til the end of time.

But that time would be ours.
And that time would be well spent
I'll thank my lucky stars
'cause you must have been heavensent.

Perpetual Motion

Love sensations running through me
High expectations when you woo me
I think I'm going out of my mind
I'm lost in love, losing track of time
But I'm winning, yes, I'm winning

It's just perpetual motion
Taking us through the night
It's an eventual potion
And we'll see that we do it right

Your body's controlling my thoughts and my actions
We tangle in love games with feelings of passion

Lonely

I thought I had a chance to win the girl
I thought happiness had come along
I guess it's my fate to be lonely in this world
My life's gone terribly wrong
Terribly wrong
Terribly, terribly, terribly wrong

Oh why? Why did this happen and how did it happen to me?
Right now, I'm the last person that she'd want to see

It's a lonely life
Such a lonely life

Friends told me the pain would cease in time
Now could anything sound more absurd?
For me the best solution is a hefty dose of wine
To keep these memories blurred
Hopelessly blurred
Hopelessly, hopelessly, hopelessly blurred

Ha Ha Ha! The whole world is laughing and I know
        they're laughing at me
Right now, I'm the last person that I'd want to be

It's a lonely life
Such a lonely life
It's so lonely, lonely, lonely
Being me

Save Yourself Some Time

Give it up, baby, read between the lines
Can't you see that our love is blind?
It's just a matter of time
And in a matter of time
You'll be mine

Our Lost Love

There's no love lost for our lost love
The skies may cry from up above
The world may end from all around
Still, our lost love will not be found

So right for you, so right for me
to live apart eternally
So hard for me, so hard for you
But hard, cold facts are no less true

In the Day

There isn't anybody
Feels like I do
I would tell everybody
'bout me and you
The tales of love I'd tell them
would all be true
In the day

In the day
Hey, hey!

And when the night comes creeping
Dark overhead
I'm glad to find you sleeping
Here in my bed
I don't remember even
One word I said
In the day

In the day
Hey, hey!

I love you in the night
I love you in the day

Life with the Bates

Brother James, he is the young one
He's almost three feet tall
And he don't know anything
About anything at all
But if you listen closely
You can hear him call
Na na-na, Na na-na, Na, Na, Na

Sister Kath plays in the backyard
with her doll there on the swing
One day she'll trade her doll in
For a certified diamond ring
But until that day comes
You can hear her sing
Na na-na, Na na-na, Na, Na, Na

Mr. Bates comes home from work late
He knows dinner's ready soon
He greets his wife with kisses
Before he heads off to his room
And while he changes his clothes
He sings this happy tune
Na na-na, Na na-na, Na, Na, Na

Mrs. Bates is in the kitchen
Treats ground beef like filet mignon
And while she serves up dinner
She sings a little song
And before you know it
The Bates all sing along
Na na-na, Na na-na, Na, Na, Na
na-na, Na, Na, na-na, Na

Everything

A girl like you is one in a million
and I don't want to let you go
There's something that you should know
Some feelings that I want to show

It's times like these when I get feeling easy
Got some loving on the way
And, girl, I want to play
But first I have to say

You mean everything to me

So tell me, tell me, tell me you love me
Like I—I love you
Tell me we've got a chance
With a love that's rare and true
Cuz I need you now
and how I need you now
Girl, can't you see

You mean everything to me
You're everything to me

Smile

Smile and the world smiles with you
Live and the world will live too
Love and the universe does the same
Try to bring some joy into a world of misery
Making this a better place for all to live
With just that little smile that means so much to so many
Watch it spread and multiply
You'll be glad if you do
So give that smile

Professor Wade,

   Your class was extremely influential and impactful on my life. I appreciate the enthusiasm and knowledge you infused into my work. With one exception (Pieces) pages 99-102 are all poems I wrote for your class all those years ago. I can't thank you enough.

                    Warmest regards,

Made in the USA
San Bernardino, CA
16 January 2018